the Goat Songs

PREVIOUS WINNERS OF THE VASSAR MILLER PRIZE
IN POETRY

Scott Cairns, Founding Editor
John Poch, Series Editor

Partial Eclipse by Tony Sanders
Selected by Richard Howard

Delirium by Barbara Hamby
Selected by Cynthia Macdonald

The Sublime by Jonathan Holden
Selected by Yusef Komunyakaa

American Crawl by Paul Allen
Selected by Sydney Lea

Soul Data by Mark Svenvold
Selected by Heather McHugh

Moving & St rage by Kathy Fagan
Selected by T. R. Hummer

A Protocol for Touch
   by Constance Merritt
Selected by Eleanor Wilner

The Perseids by Karen Holmberg
Selected by Sherod Santos

The Self as Constellation
   by Jeanine Hathaway
Selected by Madeline DeFrees

Bene-Dictions by Rush Rankin
Selected by Rosanna Warren

Losing and Finding by Karen Fiser
Selected by Lynne McMahon

The Black Beach by J. T. Barbarese
Selected by Andrew Hudgins

re-entry by Michael White
Selected by Paul Mariani

The Next Settlement by Michael Robins
Selected by Anne Winters

Mister Martini by Richard Carr
Selected by Naomi Shihab Nye

Ohio Violence by Alison Stine
Selected by Eric Pankey

Stray Home by Amy M. Clark
Selected by Beth Ann Fennelly

Circles Where the Head Should Be
   by Caki Wilkinson
Selected by J. D. McClatchy

Death of a Ventriloquist
   by Gibson Fay-LeBlanc
Selected by Lisa Russ Spaar

Club Icarus by Matt W. Miller
Selected by Major Jackson

In the Permanent Collection
   by Stefanie Wortman
Selected by Chad Davidson

Other Psalms by Jordan Windholz
Selected by Averill Curdy

Booker's Point by Megan Grumbling
Selected by Morri Creech

Ornament by Anna Lena Phillips Bell
Selected by Geoffrey Brock

the
Goat Songs

James Najarian

WINNER 2017 VASSAR MILLER PRIZE IN POETRY

University of North Texas Press, Denton, Texas

Permissions:
University of North Texas Press
1155 Union Circle #311336
Denton, TX 76203-5017

The paper used in this book meets the minimum requirements of the American National Standard for Permanence of Paper for Printed Library Materials, z39.48.1984. Binding materials have been chosen for durability.

Library of Congress Cataloging-in-Publication Data

Names: Najarian, James, 1965- author.
Title: The goat songs / James Najarian.
Other titles: Vassar Miller prize in poetry series ; no. 25.
Description: Denton, Texas : University of North Texas Press, [2018] |
   Series: Number 25 in the Vassar Miller poetry prize series | Winner Vassar
   Miller Prize in Poetry, 2017.
Identifiers: LCCN 2017043653| ISBN 9781574417173 (pbk. : alk. paper) | ISBN
   9781574417258 (ebook)
Subjects: LCSH: Pennsylvania--Poetry. | LCGFT: Poetry.
Classification: LCC PS3614.A5728 A6 2017 | DDC 811/.6--dc23
LC record available at https://lccn.loc.gov/2017043653

The Goat Songs is Number 25 in the Vassar Miller Poetry Prize Series

The electronic edition of this book was made possible by the support of the Vick Family Foundation.

Cover and text design by Rose Design

For my parents and teachers

Contents

III The Devout Life

Acknowledgments

America: The National Catholic Review: "Amaryllis." *Ararat:* "Armenian Lesson," "A Map of the Old Country." *Borderlands: Texas Poetry Review:* "The Swimmers." *The Cape Rock 42.2:* "Paperwhites." *Christianity and Literature/SAGE Publications:* "Still Life." *Collective Brightness: LBTIQ Poets on Faith, Religion, and Spirituality Sibling Rivalry Press:* "Church on the Block." *Connecticut River Review:* "A Dry Season." *Folio:* "An Introduction to the Devout Life," "Resilience." *Frost Farm Poetry Prize 2016/ The Hyla Brook Poets and the Trustees of the Robert Frost Farm:* "The Dark Ages." *The Gay and Lesbian Review:* "A Farewell to the Male Body." *Jacaranda Review:* "The Bodies of Men," "Taking the Train to Reading, PA." *The Literary Imagination: Oxford University Press:* "The Frat Boys," 18.1; "From the Armenian Quarter" 18.1, "Kleptomania" 17.3. *Lay Bare the Canvas; New England Poets on Art:* "Famous Painting," as "The West Wind, Appledore." *The Mennonite:* "Longed-For Rain." *Primary Point,* "On His Blindness." *National Poetry Review,* "Last Poem About the Farm." *New Zoo Poetry Review:* "Family Visit." *Poem:* "Barcarolle," "To the Fields." *The Powow River Anthology:* "Armenian Lesson," "Goat Song." *Sandy River Review:* "Armenian Song." *Southern Poetry Review:* "Black Walnuts, November." *Sulphur River Literary Review:* "Kempton, PA After My Death." *Tar River Poetry:* "My Big Head." *Watershed:* "Near Apex, PA," "Schoolhouse: Stony Run, PA." *West Branch:* "With the Herd." *White Crane:* "My Big Head," "Travelogue" (reprinted).

Berj and Annie Chekijian must be credited for the story behind "From the Armenian Quarter."

the Goat Songs

I Armenia, PA

Goat Song

You never had just one. We had forty,
and no one ever went without a name.
To this day, in my family's photo albums
the people have been butted out by goats.
"There's Bippy," we cry out, "There's Charmian."
In general they had attractive names
that you would hesitate to give your daughters:
Candy, Ceffie, Bambi, Serenade—
or sometimes a descriptive sobriquet:
Velveeta, for a chubby orange doe;
Regina, for her royal roman nose;
Frisbee, for one who leapt all fences, teaching
a trip of young does how to follow her.

In their eyes, everything was ready to be tasted.
They thrived on poison ivy, stinging nettle,
corn stubble, honeysuckle, chickweed, bark.
They would gnaw holes in your sweaters, gulp pages
of a book. (One gobbled up a tarpaulin.)
They had selves without self-consciousness;
their gestures celebrated their desires:
the teeth they showed off when they were content
making them grin like happy, hairy gators.
How they would squat to pee, at any time
completely unaware, as an example,
that they were watering your sneakers. How they

would line up to be petted, then afterward
your hands would be veneered with several layers
of fragrant grime. Their ears, like flesh-lined felt.
Their constant rheumy burping. The shit-and-lemon
cologne they carried on them. How they hated
two things above all: being alone, and rain.
Most memorably, their eyes, which spun
in almost separate orbits. Their pupils
opened horizontally, like trestles
bestowing them a sideways *Weltanschaung,*
exquisitely contrived for sabotage:
feed bins to ransack, latches to undo,
hayracks to get stuck in, pails to overturn.
They broke though fences, scorned electric wires,
obliterated gardens. When you found them
They rubbed their heads on you for gratitude.

But goats live only six or seven years.
In our herd, they seemed to die unceasingly
like heroines from nineteenth-century opera—
of mysterious, long-thought-curable diseases:
"Milk Fever," Abscess, Bloat, "Flash Toxin." Their deaths
were harrowing; they moaned and knew their going,
and they exhausted us. My mother sold
the strongest, leaving two beloved does,
our pets. The old goats home, we called it.

Now they cameo and gambol through my sleep
gluttoning blissfully somewhere unreachable,
or padding after me through fragrant hills.
I start up in my wide suburban bed,
patting the mattress, hoping they are real,
and call the names that seem to be for strippers:
Candy, Ceffie, Bambi, Serenade.
Just as the names come out, I understand

them decades—caprine generations—gone,
leaving me only with a kind surmise:
that somewhere their uncountable-great grandkids
are cramming their mouths with rose and thistle, breaking
out of other pastures, with some other boy.

Near Apex, PA

The Kittatiny, the "Running Mountain,"
divides this country with its slack axe,
lopping the hemlock from the oak,
Slav from German, farm from quarry.

You could climb the moist road to the top;
if you fail to glimpse the emptied farms—
their crooked orchards and stands of lilac—
so much would remain within your reach.

You could take hold of it all right now.
With each of your breaths, the rose hips swell.
Pin cherries threaten to release themselves.
Hickory nuts scattergood the mud,

still green, untouched by plow or harrow.
This is the fruit of your own country:
made ready for you, but omening
another earth, off the branch, everywhere.

Armenian Lesson

with refrains from *Gulian's Armenian Grammar*, 1904

Speaking, one grants its gutturals to the air:
intimate, prolific hard h's and j's—
sounds for the kitchen, meant to bear
advice, instruction, succor, and homilies
The quieter a life, the happier it is.

On paper, its trampled circles, squat wings,
and curlicued ladles can only convey
spoken embroidery—a collection of things
you seldom have occasion to say:
The Count and Countess are in York today;

coachman, gooseberry, or *sealing-wax.*
The grammarian carefully arranges the letters
in sample sentences whose slight effects
predict none of this country's coming disasters:
Each boy has received seven piastres.

We are expecting too much from this tongue—
more than thirty-eight letters can give.
No living language could ever be strong
enough for those it could not save.
The Turkish soldiers are very brave.

Family Visit

The director remembers us well.
He hands me a complicated map,
of curves, hills, and cul-de-sacs. As on

the moon, every bump has a name. We're
the only Armenians in town,
as usual. But our view is good:

a clear lawn convenient to the road.
I did not expect the days on each stone—
just the years. Grandmother, grandfather,

grandson: my brother. You still stand out,
your dates a ribbon of only twenty years.
I have brought flowers, always the good son—

and sticks of incense, my own gesture, one
this family, Protestants all, could not admire.
The wind is coming up. My bouquets are

clumsy. I should have bought them potted.
My incense refuses to burn.
I fetch water in a plastic urn

and wash our stones. Stained and pitted,
they will never get completely clean.

Schoolhouse: Stony Run, PA

It went for twenty thousand at auction,
just too battered to make us a home.
The last owner used it to store necessities:
sawhorses, creosote, phosphate, and tar.
A stain on the floor mimics a country

we might have found in our geography textbook.
The boards will have to be taken up,
and septic put in, as blackbirds are swirling
in and out of the divided outhouses,
paying no attention to the signs "Boys" and "Girls."

We could fill the stove with wood, or coal more likely,
or scramble the thin ladder to the bell tower
as some boy had to every morning.
The bell has since been sold to a dealer
with the tiny desks and a few old maps.

Though no one will ever do sums here again,
or elocute a selected passage,
someone thought we had something to learn.
A ribbon of faultless cursive examples,
tacked to the top of the fractured blackboards,

models perfection for our truant eyes.
The elaborate F's and O's especially
seem to belong to a forgotten tongue.
In the same hieroglyph, someone has written
"Good-bye. June, 1951."

Genealogy

The year that RFK and King were shot,
your father bought the last two hundred acres
from the youngest daughter of the German family
that tilled these hills for two fat centuries.
They'd built a barn, plain red (though when it rains,
the shadows of proud horses, names, and banners
push through the damp and show themselves), and added
a wooden summer kitchen to the house,
and earlier, the year of Gettysburg,
a set of rooms with foot-thick walls of rock.
Its core was laid by the Moravians
before the Revolutionary War,
they cleared the woods and tilled between the stumps,
put up a church—of which there is no trace,
not even a shallow, naked spot—and dug
a graveyard—now an unplowed bite of field.
The stones were carted off some years ago.
The Brethren whom they named remain in rows,
eroding as we speak, down to the ones
who died in combat with the Indians,
the Lenape, in the struggle for this land—
before those clans were flung beyond the ridges,
to Indiana, Kansas, and at last
to desiccated Oklahoma, dropping
the arrowheads that show like rocky shoots
at plowing, and the tonguing names of waters—
Saucony, Maxatawny, Tulpehocken.
A hundred people speak that language now.
What was this place before that time? The glaciers
palmed each valley, seam, and gully, leaving

the brittle tiers of greasy shale impressed
with the remains of vanished beasts and flowers.
Viewing them by the pond your father cut
is like perusing grimy photographs:
these are your ancestors, the trilobites—
your cousins, the bits of carapace and leaf
from when this farm took up the ocean floor.
But before that, where was this scrap of land?—
The universe could have been no more than
a pebble, cinder, or a grain of clay:
the black dot in your uncreated eye.

Taking the Train from Kempton, PA

Start at the gift shop, once Kempton's station,
and buy a postcard:
our tan hills are retouched a gentle green.

The tourist line steams its foreshortened way
three miles to the north,
then snaps back home, like a bad idea

or a well-trained hound. Turn your back on it.
Face the unused tracks.
They bask like snakes in the feed-mill's lot

and roam unregarded behind back yards.
So skirt a black wall,
follow the shallow creek, and head for the woods—

where no trains have ventured since forty-eight,
and where, under leaves,
anthracite cinders yield fragments of light.

Down below, the creek overtakes its rocks.
When you were a kid
you were warned never to walk on the tracks.

Mayapples crowd the edge, where you should be.
Is that dull rumble
only a tractor on the new highway?

Yes. Holes in the ties gape to the water.
The pins have rusted
and slipped down the bank. It doesn't matter.

Wet jewelweed sifts through the ladder of track,
and ahead, in light,
a shed peeks out from its habit of burdock:

a washed-out brown, big as a standing man,
with a pointed roof.
A bright plate proffers the name of a town:

NORTH ALBANY. There are a few houses—
no people quite yet—
aluminum chairs on the white porches,

Ford pickups, a dog barking, schemes toward life:
a pocket of air.
You almost don't see that the tracks are cut off,

But they are, letting the dry cinder path
smudge the hills to town.
You could trace it all the railless way south—

only someone has chalked "No trains today"
in the tiny shed,
and the sky rides up, lime-bright and empty.

First Kidding

When it is time, your doe will heave herself
and murmur to an absence felt behind her.
She will notice you, although she has
no need for you. Her amniotic sac
will swell like a translucent pear and burst,
and you may glimpse a muzzle, already with
what seems a minute caprine grin, a tongue
over the tips of tiny ivory hooves.

Now she will scream, in effort, not distress.
With one last howl her vulva will unloose
a neck, then forelegs, withers, chine, and rump
down to the little sickles of the hocks.
The kid soon tries its feet—then wiggles, shakes,
unfolds, and seems at once to jig and cry.

Here is the ancient scent of fruit and wet;
it is where you come from. Cradle the kid,
towel off the veil of mucus lined with blood,
then coat the stub of cord with iodine,
staining the kid with its first man-made mark.
Take it to a teat to get what has been
gathering for these five months. Now go.

Go home. A doe will recognize her own.

Kempton, PA After My Death

Slow down. The turn in from the valley
will be as blind as ever. The tracks
no train has troubled for decades
will make you brake for them even now.

There still won't be a church in town,
and the houses, all forty of them,
will seem to want to shift their places,
like children in school. The post office,

built in 1985, will still be "new."
The sign-painter's will be there,
the feed mill, the hotel-and-tavern,
the long-shuttered farrier's, and general store.

Will the hills be greener then? I promise you
nothing. When you drive up to the old trails,
the mountains—Hawk and Pinnacle—
will stand like cast-iron cutouts on the sky.

Black Walnuts, November

The black globes could be filled with ashes.
They pox the paths to the vacant fields,

oozing a rank and sour dye.
If you were to handle one

your fingers would be tainted for a week—
as orange as embers, or a spoiled gourd;

and if you stripped the clammy rind
from the fretted shell inside, and cracked

that skull between two slabs of slate
to sift the splinters – what would you get?

The hard, bitter, and sustaining nut.

My Big Head

Let's say I was three, or maybe four
when I got my big head trapped
in the iron railing that lined our porch.
Let's say I was three. Let's say it was
September, 1968
in Wyomissing, Pennsylvania.
I was not thinking of the War,
Chicago, or the Election, but
of creeping, newt-like through its bars
—I have no idea why. I went
head-first—or forehead first, but big head
last, and wriggled, caught like a grub.
I feel it on my temples now:
My head an ear of corn in tongs.
What happened next? My brothers must
have pushed, or pulled, my mother too.
of course I'm crying now, and probably
screaming (I did both well, and often)—
not out of pain, but out of shame.
All of our neighbors, from blocks around,
stroll out of shrubbed-in yards to look at
Me. Adults, children, dogs and cats—
they're fascinated by the mushroom
head that has me. Mr. Adams,
who has a well-known tire shop
and better-known, enormous arms
tries to bend back the bars. No doing.
His biceps are the size of my
stuck head and are tattooed—
illuminated, like Bible pages—and

he smells like gasoline—all this
I notice, while the iron doesn't
budge. Somehow, a neighbor girl
Comes up with a plan. I know her—
she's somebody's au pair, named Zin.
Big girl. From Korea, but half Russian:
to me she's vast, Siberian,
even bigger than my head.
Zin laves my head with green detergent—
Palmolive, I'm sure—to make it slick.
My mother coaches. Mr. Adams
tugs at and shoves my poor beslimed
bewildered head and then I'm free,
the slippery cork (my head)—pops out.
and then I'm nestled in Zin's arms.
My mother rinses green goo off my head—
(though if you ask her now, she will
deny this ever happened.) And then?
I don't remember. Zin stayed on
A few more months. She once gave me
a bite of the seaweed that she ate.
It came in rolls, like paper towels,
and tasted null, of nothing, of
exactly not a thing. We moved
away. Mr. Adams—I don't know.
Those people watching? They're still here.

On His Blindness

The crows spatter the spent meadow:
crushed grasses and cut goldenrod.
Dark water gathers in hoof-marks,
leaving them gaping and sour as mouths.

In a moment, the crows tangle and scatter
like a black pot shot in the air.
They throw their scene against a stone—
then, in one instinctual motion

the crows contract to a single tree.
There they tense, like fingers in a fist—
Ashes, bright in the beautifying eye.

To the Fields

On the oldest maps, a township lane.
On the topographical, a set of dashes.
The road climbs the ridge behind our farm

through a land that can only be deciphered.
Shreds of wire on rotted posts
signal fields that must have been pastured

before my lifetime, and beyond that
I recognize each planting in turn:
the malachite of winter wheat,

the dull olive of a plot left fallow.
A bend evades six disputed acres,
then dips where swine were loosed to wander.

This road traverses my own history:
sweaty foraging with flocks of women,
sifting for dandelion first, then raspberry,

blackberry, and the rough leaves of the grape,
to be made into dishes strange to this land—
a great-aunt reminiscing how she picked

mulberry leaves for the silkworms of Cairo.
Her practiced hands could trace the map
of an ancient country over this one.

But I am taken past even her decades.
A pile of rocks marks out a house
where old-timers told us the still fell in.

Its barn stands solid as a pyramid,
with walls the brown of a good loaf,
every chiseled and squared-off stone

holds though the mortar—not much more
than mud—long ago leached to the creeks.
Here the road turns to its own wilderness:

a tabernacle of apple and vine,
to lead to the hill's untillable crest,
where each oak unearths a garland of rock

—sandstone, sometimes lined with quartz.
I am beyond cartography, in a realm
of instinct and sepia, and I know only

where the bare road goes, and how
it deltas among the ordinary trees.

Longed-For Rain

For weeks, the soil translated into dust,
then lint, then ash, and at last
to smoke. The creek compressed

itself to an unwilling path of stone.
Its stain lined the valley's span.
Lamb's quarter slumped in the lane.

Then, in an afternoon, the sky grew dim,
trembling with an ancient hum.
In the pool of Siloam

I wiped my useless eyes of grime and spit.
The ears unbuckle, and the eyes unbolt.

With the Herd

Late in the afternoon, the goats ascend
the stubbled hills in strictest precedence:
first, the "queen," the strongest of the does,
then each goat in order of her rank,
trailed by her skipping kids, then yearlings,
and at the end the old, complaining ones.
The herd will linger near the tractor paths
nimbly lipping kernels from bare roots,
craning their earthbound necks for maple leaves,
dowsing for dandelion and dock. Most evenings
they return, in the same, now satiated line.

But some days, the riches are too much for them;
they squander hours with their relentless mouths.
The sun drops anonymous into the damp
and they find themselves abandoned in blind fields—
while you, indoors, are waiting for the thump
of their returning hooves—and hearing nothing.
You must give up on your accustomed walls
to hoof and blunder through the black alone.
Flashlight in hand and calling to no answer,
you shine your flimsy beam on forest edges,
illuminating vines and sumac, until
you stumble on them unexpectedly—
silent and watchful, clustered in a circle,
the nannies fortressing the kids within,
just as their ancestors must have, outside
the tents of Ishmael or Abraham.
Stop calling them. Stand still. They will not stir
until you turn the light on your known face,

their weak eyes recognize and understand.
Now, rising as a body, they will follow you,
grateful and hushed as only they can be.
Together, you will find your way back home.

Last Poem About the Farm

Dusk. Color draws back from the eye.
The earth paces from alloy to alloy.

The gravel I tread, a side of barn,
the ridge that only locals name—

glisten like something galvanized.
Even the field I stumble through—

minutes ago, it offered soybeans
punctured by witch-grass and touch-me-not;

now it is only a plot of pewter.
Each oval leaf is cast in sand.

Fireflies mete out their bits of pyrite:
the only color here, a flicker that

returns in a window of the house below—
a light in a casket of tarnished plate,

where my mother wheels herself
half-inch by quarter-inch, to bed.

II Kleptomania

The Frat Boys

Their shirtless bodies are frolicking again—
tackling each other in an April storm,
spendthrift with themselves, as only young men
can be. But it is not remotely warm.

The lawn is a snarl of pectoral and arm
in a game I cannot play, or even grasp.
However rough it seems, they mean no harm,
shoulder on shoulder in a perfect clasp

of biceps, deltoid, butt, and leather ball.
I want at once to gaze and be struck blind,
though it is not these boys I want at all.
At forty-four, and taken back, I find

myself once more with Adam S. and Marty A.—
strong-featured Adam, Marty blond as Thor—
in the prepschool showers after class. They play
wet, naked soccer, and do not keep score.

Fuzz dirtying my belly and my thighs,
I was no ephebe, even at sixteen.
I lacked the ease of any of these guys,
then and now. And who could have foreseen

that Marty's chest, lamp-bright and just as clear,
along with each lithe feint and kick recalled,

would be squandered in a car crash in a year.
When last seen, Adam was aggrieved and bald.

It is not their bodies, but their carelessness
I marvel at, and these young men display.
I never will be able to possess
Adam and Marty capering in the spray.

The Bodies of Men

Like souls, they are seldom without flaw,
but swerve from the ideal in the way
water glances a shoulder or breast—

making one feel flesh with the eyes.
The bodies of men hold their desire back
longer than any hand could, and more tightly;

yet they are often found out at the end,
as a story's moral is hardly sudden,
but something you understood since you were small.

Covered or not, the body always appeals.
The desires of men reach out like tongues
and touch, as men might not. And like hair,

they appear in the most surprising places.
Desires are the body's attendant graces.

Paperwhites

They were never tentative. From the start,
the bulbs were ready to burst in our palms,

like figs fresh off the tree. They thrived on nothing,
on gravel or sea-glass; on beads and air.

Their leaves elongated by the hour,
bud-pods waking while we slept.

Soon, periscoping over the green,
they burst in a coronet of asterisks,

white upon white, summoning innocence,
but for their scent—

the odor of honey drizzled on carrion.
The house swam in their intricate potion.

We lumbered and quarreled in it, until
the soft stars collapsed on themselves

and we plucked the bulbs from their slimed glass bed.
They had given out tentacles, and were new creatures.

We snapped their stems, and immured them
deep, deep in the trash. Disgusting now,

they would never have a second season.

Travelogue

Our travel papers are seldom in order.
We lack a visa, or the proper stamps.
More often than not, we're stopped at the border,

our documents held to the light, just like this.
Our endorsements are in the wrong color ink,
our signatures void, our persons suspicious.

This isn't the first time we've been refused entry.
You are a country we will never visit.
We view your coast from a deck on the sea,

or get a hold of photographs, somewhere.
The kind of pictures that reveal no mysteries—
cloudy landscapes taken from the air.

They tell us nothing we're not meant to know.
No one responds to calls at the consulate.
There's no national airline or tourist bureau.

You are a nation whose borders are closed:
a tiny state in the hills, like Bhutan.
The ridges and valleys stay unexposed.

Or you are a gap on the map of the world;
your body, a continent, could be Antarctica—
cool, pale, and barely explored.

It could be perilous—the Khyber Pass,
a place without settlers—the Serengeti,
or a place found only on a prewar atlas

where half the globe is either pink or blue,
Ubangi-Shari, or Bechuanaland,
or someplace even harder to get to:

Cathay, Cibola, Lemuria, Mu.

Kleptomania

Start simply. Thieve small.
And stay on the ball.
Take nothing that matters—
     lost screws, ticket stubs, French fries from platters.

Now steal something better:
a breath or a letter.
Then take someone's time.
     Practice makes perfect, and the perfect crime.

Then swipe the covers,
(the names of old lovers
will give you some tips).
     Kisses for others you take on the lips.

Loot tongues for secrets—it's
using your wits,
and occasions abound.
     Astounding what people leave lying around!

Why not go on?
Be a Pro of a Con—
filch a heart for a day.
     As soon as you're done with it, throw it away—

or keep it for longer.
Your skills will get stronger.
Who's keeping tabs?
     Everything, everyone, is up for grabs.

In Drought

I

Blackberries dwindle to hard black caps,
knobs, bullets, stone versions of themselves.
Heat truncates the eyes of grasses.
The leaves of the grape tremble, exhausted.

Dry fruit mocks the mode of desire.
Ripe color cringes, dull on the vine,
in a berry's shape. Yet no matter how hard
it is in the mouth, each fruit cries

Berry, Berry, to the juice-filled eye.

II

The heart, too, has come to fruit in drought.
It longs to burn on the peak's spare edge
in the way that gold, dark inside its hill,
must yearn for air. Yet the heart is aware
of the small terms it lives by,

its few words diminishing.

Mnemonic

My hands are now a monument to your body.
My shallow bowl of palm secures a place
a place that only I know, low on your thigh,
Like a well-cast hinge, the letter's envelope,
a puzzle waiting for its misplaced piece.
Think of the spots these hands memorialize—
your hip's quick pivot, your sweat's salt rivulet—
they placed their cushions on your belly's divan,
or grasped the curve of your cheek, or cupped a knee.
The fit was perfect, like arithmetic.

The heart has chosen not to think at all.
Caged in the body, it does not look back.
Nor does the mind. At most, the mind recalls
a color, or some tunes. If it had its way
the mind would shrink its memory down to a ball,
and spin, unique, a bead in a pearl-lined shell

of skull. It is the body that remembers.

Head of Amenhotep III, "Possibly a Forgery"

Brooklyn Museum

He is all helmet,

polished to a despot's adored black sheen.
This man would look out of place on the street:
his marks of station

meaningless now. As for his attitude?
Four thousand years have not opened his eyes.
Untouched, unfevered,

his lips have parted for no one else's.
His corpse was cured for his soul to visit,
but the soul endures.

If the body rots, it can use a spare—
a statue—or in a pinch, just a head.
Pharaoh's pied à terre

in this world might well be a forgery.
He would be grateful for a counterfeit,
for any proxy.

Amenhotep could be in Brooklyn now,
revolving in his theocratic fraud.
Who would ever know?

Against Desire

The hand remains outside the body it caresses.
It gives out. It will always become
somebody else's
thigh, pectoral, or even palm.

The tongue, despite what it says,
will slacken, and recover its control;
in seconds or days
it draws back to its plush shell

and even the eye retreats from color,
shutting its door on a delightful scene—
that of another
desiring eye, and its helpless man.

So why bring up the old fact of desire?
A rock waiting for a ship to wreck,
it is always there.
Or, an attentive student of music,

it is eager to break out its squeaky violin
and play a song for us that is still familiar.
We know the tune—
the words, though, we no longer remember.

The Hands of an Ex-Lover

I no longer lay claim to them.
I remember hands cool and white,
clumsy at night,

blind fish ripening in a cave:
each finger paler than
its core of bone—

lilies, opening in a dim room.
They were unmarked and empty
until the day

I carved the knuckles in low relief,
hollowed the palms with my own,
and I began

to turn your fingers on the lathe of my arm.
to etch the lines on your wrists' marble.
Barely visible

now, they have been worn down
by an unknown
finger or tongue.

Whose labor have these hands become?
They are warm, and stronger
than I remember,

yet white as ever—as in my day, when
your hands were made of pearl.
Now they are metal.

A Farewell to the Male Body

There is no guidebook to this country.
Hardly anyone ends up here.
The borders are guarded, and very secure.

The duty is high, and the customs, difficult.
There's not much for a tourist to do,
but settle down. We were just passing through,

taking in the sights: the cheeks, the hair.
We saw the eyes, a well-known resort.
The mouth, the only really free port,

was closed. For the rest—well, let's just say
from the neck on, it was all downhill.
There's no time to go over it all—

the shoulder's monument and arm's peninsula
pivot their strength to the unwarmed sea.
The arm's thin grain rolls gently on the way.

Very strange: we thought we saw mountains.
There were five, in the distance, or so we'd heard.
But as we approached them, they disappeared

and we were on the other side of the world,
in a treeless valley, misnamed the palm:
a place to which tourists sometimes come

to shake hands with the country's only inhabitant.
A very nice man, you could meet him anywhere.
Remember me to him, if you get that far.

III The Devout Life

Church on the Block

The seller's agent shepherded our crew
past granite pillars to an interior
frou-froued in ivory, gilt, and baby blue.
It seemed at once part chapel, part boudoir.
The agent let us see what we could see.
She recognized what we had come there for—
each of us both neighbor and voyeur:
something happened in the rectory.

We thumbed the altar, tried the priest's huge chair,
strolled through the sacristy—a disarray
of brass and velvet: chalices dropped where
they were, half-crated in a passageway,
vestments still hanging. It was like Pompeii—
as if the dwellers made off suddenly
as we walked in, as if that very day
something happened. In the rectory

We lost ourselves, meandering in a den
of closets opening to libraries,
to lounges, nooks, and burrows, and again
to closets. A boy could crawl around for days,
trapped in its perfect, secret-making maze.
Though the priests' house was torn down eventually,
the church remains, apartments now, and says:
something happened in the rectory.

The Dark Ages

I

For years, my mother shuttled from her garden
to the stove, from barn to sewing room to sons,
her life like an unopened work of history.
Then came the silences. Was she tired? Bored?
She hovered in her kitchen the whole day.
Skillets and glassware tumbled from her hands,
her face a cast of lead. Her garden shrank
to towering, weedy greens and wiry vines.
We did not plow it for the coming year.

II

Late Roman Britain had begun to turn
even before the soldiers were withdrawn.
With the seas unguarded, little was brought in.
Ale and lard replaced Rome's wine and oil.
The towns dispersed, as townsfolk headed to
the countryside to try the earth. At first,
the city fathers decently tore down
deserted baths and temples. Villas crumbled.
Those who stayed grew barley in the ruins.

III

She had trouble walking, or rather starting
walking—her feet seemed bolted to the ground,
the brain not ordering its provinces.

She spoke a rote "no, thank you"; rarely "yes."
Her kingdom dwindled to a bed and toilet—
a quilt she planned still hanging from the wall,
bright calicoes once basted to white flannel,
seed-packets, knitting, quiet as offerings—
her life now archaeology around her.

IV

Eventually, Rome took its army home.
With Rome went every skill. The coarse pots made
in native kilns, declined, then disappeared.
Foundries halted, and with them nails vanished.
The people foundered barefoot in the mud
as shoes could not be made—or coffins either.
The dead were thrown directly in the ground.
Silt clogged the cities' sewers. Canterbury
dwindled to a pasture, York a marsh.

V

In daylight she may keen for hours, unaware.
All night she shrieks, but does not hear her sounds.
She grips a toy she's had since she was small,
a drowsy chimpanzee whose eyelids close.
Nurses have put her in a safe low bed.
Half-buried in her sheets, she is a baby
lost in a little boat. She knows my name,
but wails, and can't say why. At times I can
make out a single word: "no, no, no, no."

VI

The towns and villages have emptied out.
We gather in our clans amid the dregs,
atop a hill-crest or a crumbled fort,
dwelling among the hogs we kill each fall,
gorging because we cannot let them waste.
Our women scrounge for bits of bead and bronze.
They roast our gritty roots right in the fire
or cook in cauldrons dug from ancient graves,
sepulchri: pots that once held human ashes.

Resilience

I

The lake has lost grip of its geese. Their dark specks
no longer stipple a darker mirror.

The cattle rustle in the calamus
as if they have somewhere to get to.

And the heart, the perennial heart
that blooms and dies back down

hoards green shoots under a dry diadem.
They may flower in the spring. They may not.

II

The heart adores surfaces. A mayfly,
it grazes a pond's face, then proclaims:

"I feel. I know." Yet it only guesses.
The heart grows large on its diet of breezes.

III

Facts fall apart in your hands, yet you grip them.
You pluck numbers and hold them to the light.

They rumor other numbers, and palaces
beyond those. You set up house and live.

But with or without you, the unassured heart
lives and dies and lives and dies again.

Do not contemplate the heart.
There are places it refuses to enter.

Halcyon Days

The sky was a lovely Valium blue
as I woke feeling well.
I Adderalled my way to work,
serene as Seroquel.

I found my boss dis-Demerolled
by untouched mounds of files.
But known for my Abilify,
I Zolofted all with smiles.

I'm Zocor-hearty in a pinch,
and able to succeed.
The work just Thorazined me by
at a Strattera's speed.

Then, happy as a Vicodin,
I took a Xanax home.
I caught the sunset on my way,
a bright Mercurochrome.

I dined upon a One-A-Day,
Cialised with the wife,
and Ambiened myself to bed,
Wellbutrin with my life.

An Introduction to the Devout Life

Go on a furlough: exempt yourself
from the bric-a-brac of the affections:
from dawns, dusks, mountaintop glimpses,

desperate rocks and significant clouds.
Don't renounce them, merely see them on,
like things you choose not to buy at the moment.

The wind rustling the parched grasses—
reminding you of your private afflictions—
wouldn't trouble you in the city.

The moonlight, which seems so lucid with feeling,
isn't much more than light from the moon
shining on somebody else. It does not mean *loss*

or bring on any actual sorrow.
Take a few steps back from these sights and names;
there will be a time when you are able

to look at a particularly redolent scene
and notice the sky is no more than blue,
the grasses merely a very bright green.

Armenian Song

The woman bends the branches to the ground.
She is old enough to know an older country.

Musk-flavored, sugary, and prodigal,
the roses yield themselves. She unhooks one.

It has become a gate. At once she is
a pale girl on the Anatolian coast

before the war, before before or after,
in some remembered and hand-colored scene.

Her sisters gather poppies into baskets.
They chirp in French, and laugh into the air.

on this bright day in June, the poppies are
the reddest spots the sisters can imagine.

The Swimmers

flicker in their liquid
carousel,
        minute flaws in a blue
paste jewel,
        strings quivering a cool,
intricate
        machine. The water is
absolute,

        heartless, leaching their selves
from themselves:
        leaving them nothing but
lines and curves:
        mathematics. They have
given up
        on human air. They can
never stop.

        Barely physical, and
not like you,
        they are figures you can
never know;
        this, a rite you cannot
take part in.
        These, their bodies (almost
forgotten.)

A Map of the Old Country, with Disputed Region

entitled "Nor Hayastan [The New Armenia], 1923"

I

The village my grandfather
lived in (and fled from),
has become a series
of ciphers, next to
a thick red line.

Other people hold on
in the same beige landscape.
They eat—sparingly,
nowadays—a cuisine
sharpened by lemon and salt.

This nation has taken the shape
of a bag filled with stones,

a hare, slung on a pole.

II

Someone is mortaring villages
in the country on my wall.
The paper puckers with each hit.
Mountains wrinkle in the heat.

Men aim at one another

in a valley to the right.
Its borders are an unfortunate,
ambiguous width. Measure it—

it is no bigger than half your hand.

III

For years, the lake
in the heart of the country
has seemed to be drying up.
On the map it has left
a surprisingly delicate blue.

Still Life, Provenance Uncertain

Though the apple may be golden,
no goddess would fight over it.
It doesn't exactly shine

in the odd bowl of yellowish fruit.
Still, these globes consign
some color to the air, not quite

gilt or honey, topaz or saffron,
but another yellow entirely—
a color that says: we ripen

ourselves for your absorbent eye.
A grapefruit undoes a single tier.
A lemon loosens its astringency

inside its skin, ready to offer.
It is your moment they bear:
your ripeness they wait for.

Uncle Gustavus

"Uncle was an invalid,"
the family always said.
A valetudinarian,
he seldom left his bed.

With something wrong about his heart,
he had his separate floor,
with his own valet and nurse
in the years before the War.

Gustavus was invisible,
or at least could not be seen,
too frail to play with other boys,
he passed on at nineteen.

"A gentle boy," said Aunt Cecile,
"and always glad. He smiled
all the time." Aunt Bea agreed,
"He was our fairy child."

At hours there was no company
he'd be led down from his room
like a cherub from a cloud.
On fine days, Bill the groom

might take him for a pony ride
(always within the grounds).
What kind of invalid was Uncle?
He had Down's.

Barcarolle

I

You grow more quiet in the afternoons, and slowing,
you doze on chairs, a sofa, or a raft of bed

while holding out one hand, as if to test the waters.
Your mouth, opening, welcomes the vowels of the sea

and greets the knowledge that I did not know you knew:
how in the strange sounds sleep makes, each breath births a change.

II

The ocean, like a tongue, cannot be stilled or stopped.
It mimes the permanent, but turns with every name.

Where are the walls that keep the seven seas apart?
Their waters rustle into one another's waters

in the way that talk, unwanted, droops and loses aim.
Promiscuous, our words breed infinite demurrals—

Each word a little funeral to its intention.
the words, "I love" become, when spoken "I have loved."

III

Only a boy would play Canute against this wave.
It shatters into smaller waters on the rocks or jetty,

Its waters broken up and unnegotiable.

Famous Painting

after Childe Hassam
Yale University Art Gallery

This is outrageous. There is nothing here.
Sugary whitecaps seem to have been
dusted over a preposterous ocean—
all a relentless, candied azure,

hardening under the crayoned skies.
Blobs of vessels could be, at this distance
almost anything—galleons or junks,
dissolving under toybox puffs of cloud.

If we could sail to the prim horizon,
point our feet to its anonymous shore—
Where would we end up? Iceland or Portugal,
Madagascar, Zanzibar, or merely

Long Island. Or somewhere we will never be.
Here, then. Taste some of the sea.

From the Armenian Quarter, Jerusalem

Inside, we counted only several thousand—
the monks still seal the gates each night at ten.
Our families intermarried with our histories.
We knew who had escaped which massacre,
whose name enshrined a child or brother dead
or given up for dead,—and we shared these names.

We went by nicknames, everyone. We had
a *Hagopee Maryaam*, a "Jacob's Mary,"
to distinguish her from Joachim's or David's.
A *Hovnan*, Jonah, might be tall or cross-eyed
or someone's seventh son. A man we called
Keghatseeg Hovsep, or "Joey the Beauty,"
was a balding, pockmarked dwarf. One of thirty
Marys was known as *Anousheeg*, or "cute."
She was illiterate. During the war,
whoever read her husband's letters to her
let it be known that he addressed his wife
as *Anousheeg Maryaam*, or "Mary the Cutie"
Though she was neither plain nor beautiful,
she would be called "The Cutie" her life long.

There was a person whom we called *Shefeeya*,
an Arab Christian who chose to live with us.
Above, she was a man, below, as far
as anybody knew, she was a woman.
She had no breasts; she shaved. She wore the robe
of an Arab man, only without the headdress.
She labored in the orphanage with us,

and left the Christian Quarter for our own.
Even in that time and place, we understood:
when she sat with the men, she was treated
like a man; she idled like one, and she smoked.
When with the women, she became a woman—
gossiped, pulled dough, and did the rougher sewing.
Before I left the Quarter for this country,
I would spend evenings at canasta with her.
She played an able hand, and dwelled with those
who always lived between, among, and under:
the people who had christened her *Shefeeya*,
in Arabic: "One who must be pitied."

Amaryllis

Why did you welcome it into the house?
Numb in the coffers
of uncounted bulbs, it seemed so harmless—

blind as a doorknob, intimating green.
But coddled indoors,
it pillared overnight, and pursued the sun,

fattening its five uneven sacks of flame.
It knew our natures,
and had come to ready its own kingdom.

In the midst of our domestic exhibit,
all the souvenirs
of ceramic, brass, dyed glass, and silver plate

that we positioned for a sensuous curve or gleam
become amateurs:
the foolish gestures of the game of home.

As for our fine timbers, and careful décor—
At any moment all may break with pleasure.

Booker's Point, **by Megan Grumbling:**

"Megan Grumbling's closely observed, lyrical poems give us a fine portrait of rural Maine and of one man whose life was so intertwined with the area around Ell Pond, it is hard to imagine how he could ever have lived anywhere else."

—*The New York Journal of Books*

"Grumbling has a powerful ear for the music and rhythms of colloquial speech. She's subtle, conjures the natural world richly and convincingly, and her subject matter is surprising and intriguing. I also admire how she handles meter. Nobody else that I know of is writing like her."

—**Morri Creech**, author of *Sleep of Reason* and judge

"In *Booker's Point* Megan Grumbling introduces us to a man who nurtures his corner of the earth: he reads it, tends it, and is shaped by it in return. Such attention creates a world for the reader that is both grounded and transformative, revealing, as one poem says, how our 'elements transcend us, perfectly immersed in here.' Grumbling writes with such formal agility the poems are at once conversational, taut, and utterly vivid. The dense beauty of her language makes it palpable, makes a reader need to savor, to say the words aloud. She is Hopkins and Frost and completely herself. In an age of virtual reality, these poems call us back to something crucial."

—**Betsy Sholl**, author of *Rough Cradle*
and former Poet Laureate of Maine

"Megan Grumbling's book of poems is a gift to anyone who appreciates rich, graceful poems that tell an unforgettable story. I loved every word of this gorgeous book!"

—**Monica Wood**, author of *Papermaker*
and *When We Were the Kennedys*

Other Psalms, by Jordan Windholz:

"As though finding in Simone Weil's theology of divine absence a reason to sing, in the opening poem, 'Invocation,' the singer of *Other Psalms* discovers a vocation: to sing, perversely, eloquently, of and to silence. Ambitious and exigent, these poems are refreshingly alert to all of the formal necessities of contemporary poetry, recognizing the inadequacy of any single measure to encompass the human longing for presence."

—**Averill Curdy**, author of *Song and Error* and judge

"Jordan Windholz's *Other Psalms* harmonizes reverie and reverence. This poet recognizes 'journey and wanderings//as stemming from the same seed.' Thus the musically dense disciplines of his poems balance an irony and occasional irreverence that make *Other Psalms* vivid and not simply beautiful. In other words, this book harmonizes human and holy."

—**Elizabeth Robinson**, author of *On Ghosts* and *Blue Heron*

"There is a lushness and sonic abandon in many of these poems that reflects their devotional aspirations, 'to cradle divinity by flutter or buzz.' There is also a wryness, even causticity, completely in keeping with the apophatic side of the tradition. The paradox of religious writing, or any writing for that matter, carried out across a life's changes in circumstances and temperament, requires both extremes in order to stay vivid. A difficult balance to keep, a dangerous tightrope to walk—*Other Psalms* does it thrillingly."

—**Nate Klug**, author of *Rude Woods* and *Anyone*

In the Permanent Collection, by Stefanie Wortman:

"Intensity of heart, intensity of mind, flowering as one: Stefanie Wortman's poems redeem 'wit' back to its root meaning of 'insight' or 'vision,' the same root as the Sanskrit 'veda.' For example: the resonance of 'shades' when the words 'blind king' on a truck mean not Lear but 'installer of shades.' Or, a dance of death where the words 'trips' and 'plays' have doubled, heartbreaking and celebratory meanings. *In the Permanent Collection* merits its title."

—**Robert Pinsky**, author of *Gulf Music* and 1997–2000 Poet Laureate

"These poems seem haunted by a mostly nameless melancholia. *In the Permanent Collection*, however, turns its grim geography of prisons, mortuaries, and tawdry suburbs into something close to classical elegy. 'In sunken rooms,' Wortman writes, 'on scratchy rugs, maybe we've never known happiness.' It's that 'maybe'—the smart hedge—that renders her poems complex, often beguiling, but never without a gesture of redemption. This should be part of any serious poet's permanent collection."

—**Chad Davidson**, author of *The Last Predicta*

"In this gorgeous, self-possessed book, Stefanie Wortman doses out pleasure and pain in perfect measure, her symphonic formal skills setting us up for unexpected heartbreak. Wortman's poems look for redemption in and as art—and as such console even as they seek out consolation themselves. They are spirited and haunted, intimate and estranged. *In the Permanent Collection* is a first book by a poet who has already hit her stride."

—**Gabriel Fried**, author of *Making the New Lamb Take*

Club Icarus, by Matt W. Miller:

"A down-to-earth intelligence and an acute alertness to the gritty movement of language are what you'll treasure most in Matt Miller's *Club Icarus*. You just might pass this book on to a friend or relative who needs it, or even better yet, purchase their own copy."

—**Major Jackson**, author of *Holding Company* and judge

"In Matt Miller's deeply satisfying collection, there is a visceral longing that cannot be ignored, a surrender to the body's fate but also a warring against it. There is the tenacious blood-grief for the lost father but also the deeply abiding yet fearful love of the new father.

At the heart of these wonderful poems is a naked wrestling with all those forces that both wither life and give it bloom, those that rob us and those that save us."

—**Andre Dubus III**, author of *House of Sand and Fog*

"In a stunning array throughout Matt W. Miller's remarkable *Club Icarus* are instances of the kind of poetic alchemy that coaxes beauty and a rather severe grace out of the most obdurate materials and unlikely contexts. Here is a poet in whose artful hands language has become an instrument that enables us to know the world again and, simultaneously, as if for the first time."

—**B. H. Fairchild**, winner of the National Book Critics Circle Award for Poetry

"In *Club Icarus* the universal themes of birth and death, love and loss—are woven together with a luminous, transcendent brush. This book is a sly and beautiful performance."

—**Marilyn Chin**, author of *Rhapsody in Plain Yellow*

Death of a Ventriloquist, by Gibson Fay-LeBlanc:
"Whether he's overhearing a conversation in a tavern or the music stuck in his head, Fay-LeBlanc uses his ventriloquist to raise important questions about how we perform ourselves through language. The tension that permeates his poetry—what is seen and unseen, said and eavesdropped, true and trickery—culminates in a debut that rings out long after Fay-LeBlanc's lips stop moving."

—*Publishers Weekly* starred review

"What drives the poems in this wonderfully animated debut volume and prompts the reader's pleasure in them is the patent honesty of the poet's voice. In the 'ventriloquist' series itself, Fay-LeBlanc creates a remarkable refracted self-portrait, bristling with moments of unabashed illumination."

—**Eamon Grennan**, author of *Out of Sight*

"In the words of visual artist Paul Klee, 'art doesn't reproduce what we can see, it makes it visible.' The turf of these poems is a 'vision country' in which our narrator/ventriloquist makes visible (and audible) the world to which he restlessly attends."

—**Lisa Russ Spaar**, author of *Satin Cash* and judge

"Gibson Fay-LeBlanc is a new poet with an old voice. The ventriloquist here throws his own voice while sitting on his own knee, speaking for, but not to, himself, making magic in (and of) plain sight."

—**Brenda Shaughnessy** author of *Human Dark with Sugar*

Circles Where the Head Should Be, by Caki Wilkinson:

"Playful and soulful, buoyant and mordant, snazzy and savvy—Caki Wilkinson's poems pull out all the stops, and revel in making the old mother tongue sound like a bright young thing. Lend her your ears and you'll hear American lyric moxie in all its abounding gusto and lapidary glory, making itself new all over again."

—**David Barber**, Poetry Editor, *The Atlantic*

"*Circles Where the Head Should Be* has its own distinctive voice, a lively intelligence, insatiable curiosity, and a decided command of form. These qualities play off one another in ways that instruct and delight. An irresistible book."

—**J. D. McClatchy**, author of
Mercury Dressing: Poems, judge

"Caki Wilkinson's marvelous and marvelously titled *Circles Where the Head Should Be* contains poetry as dexterously written as any today. And beneath its intricate surface pleasures lie a fierce intelligence and a relentless imagination constantly discovering connections where none had been seen before. This is a stunning debut."

—**John Koethe**, author of *Ninety-fifth Street*,
winner of the Lenore Marshall Prize

"Like Frost, Wilkinson believes in poem as performance, showing off her verve and virtuosity. She is the 'Lady on a Unicycle,' negotiating her difficult vehicle through the pedestrian crowd with 'the easy lean achieved/by holding on to nothing'—a joy to witness."

—A. E. Stallings, author of *Archaic Smile* and *Hapax*

Stray Home, by Amy M. Clark:

Two poems from *Stray Home* were selected by Garrison Keillor, host of *A Prairie Home Companion* and of *The Writer's Almanac*, to be included in *The Writer's Almanac*, broadcast May 28 and 29, 2010.

"*Stray Home* is a great read. The poetic form found in its pages never feels forced or full of clichés. Whether you are a fan of formal verse or just like to 'dabble,' *Stray Home* is a collection to pick up."

—*Good Reads*

Ohio Violence, by Alison Stine:

"In the mind, Ohio and violence may not be words immediately paired—pastoral cornfields, football fields, and deer versus the blood and splintered bone of a fight or a death. Yet *Ohio Violence* achieves that balance of the smooth and vivid simmer of images and the losses that mount in Alison Stine's collection."

—*Mid-American Review*

"Shot through with a keen resolve, *Ohio Violence* is an arresting, despairing book that alternately stuns and seduces."

—*Rain Taxi*

"One comes away from *Ohio Violence* newly impressed with the contingency and instability of the hazardous universe that is our home; and impressed, as well, with the ability of these stark, memorable poems to distill that universe into language and to make of it a sad and haunting song."

—Troy Jollimore, *Galatea Resurrects #13*

Mister Martini, by Richard Carr:

"This is a truly original book. There's nothing extra: sharp and clear and astonishing. Viva!"

—**Naomi Shihab Nye**, author of *Fuel,* judge

The Next Settlement, by Michael Robins:

"Michael Robins' prismatic poems open windows, then close them, so we're always getting glimpses of light that suggest a larger world. With never a syllable to spare, these poems are beautiful and haunting. I know of nothing like them."

—**James Tate**, winner of the 1992 Pulitzer Prize for Poetry

"*The Next Settlement* is a finely honed, resonant collection of poems, sharp and vivid in language, uncompromising in judgment. The voice in this book is unsparing, often distressed, and involved in a world which is intrusive, violent, and deeply deceitful, where honesty and compassion are sought for in vain, and refuges for the mind are rare."

—**Anne Winters**, author of *The Key to the City,* judge

re-entry, by Michael White:

"Michael White's third volume does what all good poetry does: it presents the sun-drenched quotidiana of our lives, and lifts it all into the sacred space of poetry and memory. He delights us with his naming, but he also makes us pause, long enough at least to take very careful stock of what we have. He makes us want to hold on to it, even as it trembles in the ether and dissolves."

—**Paul Mariani**, author of *Deaths and Transfigurations,* judge

"Here is a book that explores the interplay between interior and exterior landscapes with such generous and beautifully crafted detail that readers will feel they are no longer reading these poems but living them."

—**Kathryn Stripling Byer**, Poet Laureate
of North Carolina 2005–2009